Kids' E-mail and Letters from Camp

Bill Adler, Jr.

RUTLEDGE HILL PRESS®
NASHVILLE, TENNESSEE
A THOMAS NELSON COMPANY

Published by Rutledge Hill Press, a Thomas Nelson Company, P.O. Box 141000, Nashville, Tennessee 37214.

Illustrations by Loel Barr.

Library of Congress Cataloging-in-Publication Data

Kids' e-mail and letters from camp / Bill Adler, Jr.
    p. cm.
   ISBN 1-55853-827-5
   1. Camps—Anecdotes. 2. Children's writings. I. Adler, Bill, 1956–

GV192. .K53 2000
796.54'083—dc21   00–055261

Printed in the United States of America
1 2 3 4 5 6 7 8 9—05 04 03 02 01 00

Introduction

In 1958 my father wrote *Letters From Camp*, which was published by Chilton Books. Numerous printings later, *Letters From Camp* has sold over one million copies and is regarded as a classic. *Letters From Camp* was a reflection of the idealism of childhood and sense of wonder in the late 1950s.

Now, forty years later, I have written a new volume for the twenty-first century: *Kids' E-mail and Letters from Camp.* The past four decades have brought immense changes to the world, far too numerous to list. I remember being at Camp Wildwood in Bridgton, Maine, on July 20, 1969, the day Neil Armstrong landed on the moon. That was a different era. But as much as times have changed, at least one thing has remained the same—kids still go to camp. Other things have changed: now kids have computers at camp, and there are even computer camps. Camp has gone high-tech.

However, kids still have their innocence and charm. They're still playful and curious. Only now they have high-tech means of communication that hardly anybody conceived of in 1958.

And kids still write letters home from camp. But what they say—and how they say it—is very different. *Kids' E-mail and Letters from Camp* is a collection of witty, silly, concerned, touching, fascinating, and always entertaining letters. Some of these letters, as you will see, relate to this new technology, which has permeated many summer camps, but many of the letters are about, well, camp stuff.

Bill Adler, Jr.
Washington, D.C.
www.adlerbooks.com

Don't be mad, but I can't tell what's mine when the clothes come back from the camp laundry. A lot of those little name-tag things you ironed on must have fallen off. I don't think I'm going to send any clothes to the camp laundry again. I'm just going to keep wearing the same things over and over till I get home.

Love,
Fred

Today we explored the local mountains using the counselor's neat topography CD-Rom. It showed all the footpaths to the top, and had a great GIF image of the lake at the top of the mountain, which was pretty, but the computer said that it's too cold to swim in it. Next weekend we're taking a virtual rafting trip down Sebago River.

Love,
Gabe

Does Amazon.com deliver to the woods? I'm running low on books. If they don't, I guess I could borrow some from Ellen.

Love,
Fawn

It's weird waking up to a bugle instead of an alarm clock or Daddy yelling, "Time to get up. We're late!" I wonder how the counselor who blows the bugle wakes up.

Your son (in case you don't remember),
Roy

Next summer remind me to bring a battery operated fan. Our bunks don't have electricity. But it's not as hot here as it was when we were waiting in line at Disney World, so I'm OK.

Love,
Mark

Good news! War paint comes off.

Love,
Boyd

I forgot to mention that I modified the start-up sequence on the home computer. It's going to boot directly to Tomb of Death unless you press F7 as soon as you see Starting Windows, and then press the F2 and then the F5 keys five seconds after. I'll fix it when I get back.

Would you like a candy tray or vase made out of Popsicle sticks from my arts and crafts class?

Love,
Heather

P.S. You can exit the Tomb of Death either by getting to the 6th level, or by finding the magic ring, which is sometimes hidden under a rock, and sometimes in the vulture's claws.

You'll be happy to know that we aren't allowed outside until we have sunscreen on. I have grape sunscreen, but Molly, who has the top bunk has strawberry smelling sunscreen. Two of the other kids have banana sunscreen. It's smells great in here.

Love,
Julie

One of the disks you left with me at camp isn't completely blank, so I had to erase the stuff on it to make room for my art projects. I don't think it was anything important—there were just two files I erased—marketingplan.doc and salesrevenue.doc. You have copies, right? Gotta go to the lake now. It's free swim.

Love and kisses,
Margot

Camping in the woods isn't scary, but the counselors' scary stories are very scary! I'm glad my flashlight has an alkaline battery, because I kept it on all night.

Love,
Missy

We saw a bear on our hike! It saw us, too. The bear started running before we did. Away from us, which is good.

Love,
Molly

Last night somebody tied together all the pairs of sneakers at camp. I think it was a counselor. It was a funny joke!

Love,
Betsy

There might be Wherewolves in the woods. I didn't believe it at first, but a lot of people have told me the same story.

Love,
Mark

P.S. I'll be careful.

We're learning about nature this week. Today I learned about trees, especially what happens if you lean against a tree that's making sap. The sap makes maple syrup, but it also makes you stick to the tree.

Love,
Angie

All of a sudden it started to thunder and lightning while we were swimming in the lake. They made us get out of the lake so fast! It looked like that movie where everyone runs out of the water to escape the shark. Only the lightning wasn't fake and neither was the running.

Love,
Ruth

There's a woodpecker that lives in the tree behind our bunk. He likes to get up early in the morning before revelry. So we're usually awake before revelry, too. My counselor says that the woodpecker might end up as woodpecker stew one night, but I think he's kidding.

Love,
Hope

Guess what? My counselor used to be a programmer at Apple. He's going to give us a virtual tour of the Pentagon computer next Sunday night. He said that we might also get to peek into the CIA's computer, but we're not supposed to tell anyone.

Your pal,
Donny

Even though our family are vegetarians, is it okay if I kill bugs? There are lots of muskitos and flies and I don't think you would want them eating me.

Love,
Sally

We set up a weather station. It has a barometer, thermometer, wind meter and solar meter. According to the weather station, it's going to be sunny tomorrow. If it's not sunny, I don't know what we'll do with the weather station.

Love,
Margaret

I miss you so much. The first two nights at camp I cried myself to sleep because I missed you so much. I wish I took your picture with me to camp. There's nobody here to tell me a good dream story.

I am making lots of new friends and I'm not sad during the daytime like I am at night.

But I really like this camp, so I'm glad you sent me. I just wish you could be here around bedtime.

Love,
Teresa

Tuesday is sports day. We're not allowed to turn on our computers all day.

Love,
Sarah

I've finally learned how to yo-yo! My counselor Isobel taught me during the three rainy days in a row we had. She's a great yo-yoer.

Love,
Maria

Some of the counselors play country music. It's not exactly like my B*witched and Britney Spears CDs, but I'm getting to like it.

Love,
Lindsay

When you're bad at camp, they take away your comics for a day. Good thing they don't take away your computer.

Love,
Billy

We're not allowed to use the word "whatever" at all. The head counselor said that we have to say "yes" or "no" instead, like when we have to decide between free swim or water polo. Whatever.

Love,
Vivian

Can I sleep in my sleeping bag when I get home? I've gotten used to it, and this way you don't have to wash my sheets!

Love,
Maya

Guess what we did today? We took something called a record album and used it to keep squirrels away from the birdfeeder.

We strung the record albums along the wire. It was very funny watching the squirrels walk along the wire and then kind of spin around when they got to the albums.

Could you send me some of your record albums? We need more to keep the squirrels away.

I really love camp. They have such neat stuff here.

Love,
Barb

Almost every computer magazine that we have has an America Online disk in it. Most of us already have America Online, so the head counselor said we all should start thinking up ideas for a list called "101 Uses for an America Online disk." We're supposed to have the list finished by the end of the summer.

Here's what my bunk has got so far:

1. A mirror that makes you look thinner than you are
2. Play the CD backwards to say "AOL for free"
3. Coasters
4. Replacement tops for beanies
5. Frisbees
6. Poker chips
7. String them together into a baby rattle
8. Christmas tree ornaments
9. Laser beam deflectors for jet fighters
10. Tape a lot together with duct tape to make a dress
11. Floor tiles
12. An emergency signal mirror
13. Bikini (requires four disks)

14. Wind chimes
15. Horse blinders
16. Pizza cutter
17. Wobble wedges for uneven furniture legs
18. Applause-helpers (clap two together)
19. Costume for the 21st Century version of The Tin Man
20. Dividers to help organize your *other* computer disks
21. An eye test eyecover for the optometrist
22. Belt buckle
23. Dangle earrings
24. Attach a stick and make ping pong paddles
25. Gerbil sled
26. Coffee tabletop for a doll house
27. Bicycle reflectors
28. Hotel keyrings, so guests don't lose the keys

Please write me with any ideas you come up with. The bunk that gets to 101 first gets a prize.

Love,
Jen

I dived to the bottom on the lake today! It's kind of muddy at the bottom, so I didn't find much except for gunk. But it was fun. I think I'll need my hair washed when I get home. I couldn't get all the gunk out when I tried to wash it myself. It looks kind of funny now.

Love,
Leslie

Would you mind sending me e-mail instead of calling? It's a little embarrassing when you call and they announce my name over the P.A.

I like baseball, track and field, and desserts.

Your son,
Max

On really cold days we get hot chocolate to drink. Some mornings it's so chilly that I have to wear the scratchy sweater you packed.

Love,
Hap

Jason lost a tooth. In Maine, the tooth fairy only pays a quarter instead of a dollar. How is that possible?

Love,
Barry

We saw the northern lights last night. It was the most amazing thing I've ever seen. Thanks for sending me to this camp.

Love,
Gloria

One of the kids in my bunk has allergies and gets a shot every week. I asked my counselor and he said that you can't catch allergies from somebody, so I won't need to get shots. I hate shots!

Love,
Martin

P.S. Could you ask Dr. Lee just to make sure I can't catch allergies?

There's a big turtle that's always swimming around in the middle of the lake. We call him "Jaws" because when ever someone uses the zip line over the lake, he jumps up out of the lake and tries to bite them. Now everybody does the zip line really well, and no one ever falls in.

Love,
Martina

They serve corn on the cob here all the time. I told you I should of waited till after the summer to get braces.

Love,
Sonya

We planted tomatoes. First we put the plants in the dirt. Then we put wire cages around them. Then we watered them and weeded them. Then some deer came along and ate them all up.

Love,
Quintana

This is my last letter. My laptop's battery has run out, and it's been so rainy that the solar cells can't recharge.

Love,
Will

I got the top bunk! Yay! I haven't fallen out of the bunk once, although I did fall a little down part of a mountain on a camping trip. But I'm OK. They cleaned me up with some spray and a bunch of bandaids.

Love,
Jerry

I'm making new friends. You were right. Camp is great. I think I'll stay friends with these kids for the rest of my life.

Love,
Henry

P.S. Especially the kids on my bunk.

We went to an Irish fair on Saturday. We got to hear fiddlers and drummers and do some Celtic dancing. There were sheep, goats and cows, too. I also liked the singing. I wish I was Irish.

Love,
Kyoko

A forest ranger came to talk to our group. She talked about ecology, nature and leaving the woods the way we found it. She also said we shouldn't pick up any snakes.

Love,
Angela

I love the shade more than the sun. Next summer could you send me to camp with the biggest hat you can find?

Your daughter,
Louise

Camp is great. I love cookouts and swimming in the lake.

We're having a big discussion about keeping the bunks clean. I say that sweeping mixes up dust which hurts our computers. The counselors say that we need to sweep every day or we'll get germs. You know a lot about cleaning, Dad, so what do you say?

Love,
Roger

We're putting on The Fantasticks next Thursday. I play The Girl. You can watch the play on our camp's website, www.camphaven.com/fantasticks.html. It's great. I hope you can watch, even if ER's on.

Your star,
Samantha

It wouldn't have done any good to send me to camp with a cell phone. There's no cell phone service up here. Bobby's parents sent him with a cell phone, so that's how I know.

The counselors have whistles for emergencies.

Love,
Fiona

We had writing workshop today because it rained all day. I wrote about a horrible grizzly bear that terrorized the woods around the camp and attacked the counselors. One brave camper killed the bear with a sword and saved everyone. She got a medal and a parade because she was so brave.

Love,
Penelope

P.S. I made this story up. My counselor said there are no grizzly bears in these woods.

I don't know why I have to be at this place. We have to make up our own beds and sweep up our own bunks. Why couldn't they hire some maids? I hear this camp costs a lot, but they make the kids work all the time. Next year I'd rather go with you to a nice hotel.

Love,
Elaine

Can you believe that the camp office uses already-done clipart for the announcements? They don't even draw the pictures every day by hand. I've seen the same picture of a hamburger a million times already. Maybe they need a new graphics program, or a new scanner, or a new and faster computer. Otherwise camp is great.

Love,
Stephan

We had the biggest storm last night. The thunder was so loud that our entire cabin shook. The wind was howling, too: It felt like a giant hand was shaking our bunk back and forth. But I wasn't scared a bit.

Love,
Mindy

We visited an Indian reservation last week. They did a rain dance. I think it worked too well because it's been raining at camp for the past 4 days.

Love,
Joanne

The french fries at camp are a lot better than the ones you make at home.

Love,
Amy

Today was haircut day. The barber came to camp. Now I look just like I did the day I left for camp.

Love,
Charles

We wrote a song for our bunk to sing on talent night. Here it is. The song goes to the tune of Somewhere Over the Rainbow.

Somewhere over Camp Highland
Up in Maine
There's a bunk that we stayed in
Under a shady lane.

That little bunk was known as "Pines."
And on the bunk there grew no vines.
Believe us!

That little bunk was kept so clean,
The counselors there are never mean.
Believe us!

Somewhere over Camp Highland
Up in Maine
There the campers are happy
And nobody would complain.

Somewhere over Camp Highland
Skies are blue
And the campers who go there
Love camp and each other, too.

I wrote most of the second verse myself.

Love,
Holly

It's very dark here at night. It's not so dark at home. Why is that? Nobody ever told me that it's darker in the woods. But I'm not scared because I have my flashlight.

Love,
Bobby

P.S. Could you send more batteries, just in case?

I will be home in a week. I can't wait. I miss you so much, and I miss Snoopy, too. Does Snoopy miss me? Has he been behaving and not barking because I've been gone. Could you give Snoopy a big hug for me and tell him I'll be home very soon. Also tell Snoopy that I have lots of new socks for him to play with, since I've lost so many parts of pairs.

Miss you and miss Snoopy too,
Dan

At nature workshop we collected earthworms. The nature counselor said it's okay if I bring my collection home.

Love,
Mary

One of the counselors told me that in the winter the lake freezes so hard that you can land an airplane on the lake. Can we come back in the winter and do that?

Love,
Leo

Everybody gets their own fly swatter at camp. Boy do we ever need it! Our counselor has a new game—whoever swats the most flies gets a Hershey's Kiss.

Love,
Bob

The counselors built a tree house in the tree near our cabin. It's cool! We play up there all the time, when we're not doing other things. When you visit on visiting day you can look at it, but you can't come up because we made a rule that only the junior camp kids can go in it. That keeps the big kids out. But maybe they'll change the rules for parents.

Love,
Doria

I want to have all my bunkmates over for a sleepover after camp is over. Because there's not enough room in my room, do you think Lily could sleepover at one of her friends' houses so we can use her room, too? Please let me know soon, so I can invite everyone.

Love,
Harv

Here's our Monday schedule:

7:30am ~~Reveley~~ ~~Revalree~~ ~~Revelle~~ We get up
7:45   Flag raising
7:50   Breakfast
8:20   Bunk cleanup
8:30   Inspection (except for Fridays when we have Super Cleanup)
8:45   We start to do stuff
12   (? I forget exactly when) Lunch
12:45   Rest period and letter writing
1:30   More stuff
6:00   Wash hands and dinner
7:00   Evening program
8:15   Bunk play
9:00   Lights out (including flashlights)

Saturdays and Sundays are different. I'll tell you all about them in my next letter.

Love,
Kiki

I signed up for French at camp. I didn't even know they have French at camp. It's fun and it's sort of easy, because I take French at school. Tomorrow we're going to have French food, too. I was worried it was going to be escargot, which means snails! But somebody told me it's going to be French toast. At least I hope it is.

Love,
Al

Is there a cookbook of camp recipes you can get? The food here is even better than the food at school!

I've learned how to cook hamburgers and marshmallows so I can help.

Love,
Joel

Every night we have to wash our faces before we go to sleep, and we have to brush our teeth and floss. Did you tell my counselor to have us do this? Tell the truth, please!

Love,
Clint

What's happening in the world? I don't miss knowing the news, but I just want to check that everything is all right.

Love,
Brad

Saturday and Sunday we have pancakes for breakfast. That's my favorite breakfast. I would tell you what we have for breakfast on the other days, but I forget.

Love,
T.C.

We're learning to recycle at camp. We recycle all our paper, bottles, cans, and plastic. There's no way to recycle chewing gum, but we found that gum's real good for plugging holes in the cabin.

Love,
Tony

I won eighteen ribbons on Field Day! One blue ribbon in the relay race (which means our team came in first), two red ribbons (for second place in the sack race and in the three-legged race), one green ribbon in the hopping race (for third place), and fourteen yellow ribbons in the other races (that's what you get if you don't win a blue or red or green ribbon).

Love,
Ben

P.S. The maple syrup here is really good! It comes in these big plastic barrels with a pump. It's so much better than those little tins that you order from that place in Vermont.

Is it okay if I take the laptop you loaned me on a canoe trip? We want to use it to figure out a new route through the Saco River, and nobody else's parents will give permission to use their computer on the trip.

Love,
Jamie

Here are the kids in my bunk. You should memorize this list for visiting day:

Bobby—Bobby is my best friend at camp. We share comic books.

Larry—he likes swimming the most.

Jules—he's good at archery and rifelry.

Mark—he was homesick for the first two weeks and now spends a lot of time in the nature cabin.

Tony—he's the best at sports in the bunk.

Andy—Andy snores. Otherwise he's great.

Andy—There's another Andy. Andy O. (this one) has black hair. The other Andy (Andy B.) wears glasses. That's how you tell the two apart, except that Andy O. doesn't snore.

Gavin—He always finishes his dinner first. Gavin's a little fat. (Please don't tell him I said that.)

Me—You remember Rich, your son.

Chip—He talks loud. Chip is good at soccer and baseball.

Geoff—We call him "Slinky" because he's able to squeeze through rocks that none of the rest of us can fit through.

Al—Al's from New Mexico. New Mexico is actually part of the United States.

It's okay if you don't remember everyone on visiting day.

Love,
Rich

I need a dictionary. We play Scrabble at night, and I need to be able to look up words. Please send a dictionary that's in book form because we're not allowed to use computers after 7 p.m.

Love,
Martha

There are a couple TV shows I would like you to tape while I'm away. Would it be better if I sent you the instructions on how to program the VCR or should I write to Paul to ask him if he can come by the house?

Love,
Connor

I really need more chocolate. We're running around so much that I'm almost out of energy. Please send a lot.

To give you an example, today we had baseball, a hike halfway around the lake, capture the flag and swimming. They fed us at breakfast and lunch and we're having dinner later, but more food wouldn't hurt.

Love,
Noah

Guess what? I bet you're really surprised to get an e-mail from me. I know you thought that you were sending me to a sports camp with no computers, but guess what? We get taken to town once a week and there's a cybercafe, so I can send and check my e-mail. I still like sports, but next summer could you send me to a camp that's not so old-fashioned? The camp should have baseball and soccer and camping out, but computers are good too.

Love,
Lexy

P.S. I've made some great friends here!

Can I go to a camp where they have bungee jumping or sky diving next summer? I like Camp Meadowbrook a lot, but I think I'd like a camp with a little more adventure even more.

Love,
Bruce

We have two counselors in our cabin: Mary and Eleni. Mary is from Wisconsin and Eleni is from New Jersey. It's neat how our counselors are from all over the country. Mary is also the swim coach, so we're doing lots of swimming.

Love,
Skye

I'm learning how to sail. It's very fun. Sometimes the wind doesn't blow, so I'm also learning how to paddle.

Love,
Pete

;) That's all I have time to write now.

Love and kisses,
Hannah

We're coming out with a camp newspaper next week. Our bunk is writing the story about how the canoe capsized in the lake. It's a really exciting story, but you'll have to wait for the newspaper to come out to read all about it!

Love,
Laura

I left my Cyber Tennis Pro game at home. Could you please FedEx the CD to me, or send it up by modem (if you know how). I need to practice for the tournament as much as I can.

Love,
Susan

The camp director's dog bumped into a skunk today. P-U! Most of the time we like to play with Ginger, but not today.

Love,
Carrie

You're not going to believe what happened to one of the senior counselors last night! We had a cookout and there was a big fire to roast marshmallows. The fire was so high that the flames almost touched the trees. My counselor George was adding some more wood when

Rest period is over. George says there's no more time to write letters.

Bye,
Brian

Do we have any birds and wind CDs at home? I haven't been listening to rock music all summer long. Now I'm sort of used to falling asleep to the sounds of nature.

Love,
Annie

Some of the kids are real practical jokers. We have one kid in our cabin, Mark, who's a real heavy sleeper. The other night a bunch of kids (not me!!!) carried him out on his bed and put the bed outside the cabin. Then they pulled back the covers and put some honey on his feet. When Mark woke up there were ants all over his toes. He woke up and screamed and then came in yelling. I don't think he thought it was so funny.

Love,
Patrick

P.S. I couldn't help it, but I laughed, too.

I finally learned cat's cradle. It's real fun. I've gone as far as Baby-in-a-Basket. I'll teach you when I get back. You don't have to have a cat to play.

Love,
Jessica

Today we saw bunnies on the path that goes to the main cabin. They were so cute! I don't have a digital camera (hint hint), so I can't send you any pictures, but you can see what the bunnies look like on www.cuterabbits.com.

Love,
Amy

I'm really excited about Color War. The whole camp is divided into two teams, the blues and the golds. I'm a blue. We do all the activities, swimming, track, archery, and others. The team with the most points wins. There's also a song competition but I'm not too good at singing, so my counselor told me just to lip-sync the words.

Love,
Kevin

Did you know that you can eat dirt and not get sick? I just found that out.

The all-camp competition theme this year is Klingons versus the Federation. Weren't those names used in the old Star Trek series when you were a kid?

Love,
Frank

I'm on the swim team! My stroke is breast stroke, and I'm getting fast. The practices are really hard. Here's one of the things we have to do: Instead of swimming the length of the pool, we dive in on the width, swim the width, get out, dive in again, swim, get out and do that 10 times. My arms kind of ache at the end. But the swim coach says a good racing dive is the key to winning a sprint.

Love,
Stuart

P.S. My arms are almost too tired to write.

I met a very nice girl online Saturday. She goes to Willoughby, a camp across the lake. She's agreed to meet me on a kid's forum after camp's over.

Sincerely,
Harry

All of the kids have Pentium IIIs with 950Mhz up here. I need a faster computer right away. It's an emergency! Oh, and we might go sailing tomorrow.

Love,
Glenn

Steve got a set of headphones for his multimedia computer. The whole bunk is getting more sleep now.

Your son,
Chris

There was a beautiful rainbow yesterday. It stretched across the lake and landed on the other side of Mt. Pleasant. We haven't hiked up Mt. Pleasant yet, but I bet there's a pot of gold hidden there somewhere, because that's where the rainbow went.

Love,
Danielle

Dear Dad,

Could you ask Mommy not to color her hair a different color before visiting day? It would be confusing if she did.

Love,
Harris

P.S. She can change it when camp is over to any color she wants except that I don't really like that kind of orangey-streaked thing she did one time.

Don't let Sammy touch my computer while I'm away! And he likes to chew on my Zip disks. Don't let him! He shouldn't even be in my room. If you want him to use that baby program, please get him his own computer.

Love,
Zack

Joey and Bill got care packages from their parents. Is it okay if I order a care package for myself from eToys?

Love,
Elliot

P.S. That's all the time I have to write now. I'll tell you about our hike to Glens Falls later. It was great. We scrambled up some rocks, and then stood right under the falls! You could see the water pouring out in front. Very cool! The pond below the falls has some fish in it, too.

There's a virus going around camp. It's nothing serious, but you should destroy all my e-mail after reading it so you don't catch anything.

Love,
Karen

I swam the entire length of the pool under water. I was out of breath near the end, but they didn't have to fish me out of the water like they did with Lisa.

Love,
Nancy

Today was our first day at archery. It's okay, but not as fun as Target Master Pro. Even though I can hit the target more with real arrows, sometimes the bow string slaps my arm and that hurts. Target Master Pro never hurts.

The rest of camp is great. I especially like swimming.

Love,
Jan

If we don't write a letter home, we don't get dessert. I thought you should know.

Love,
Keith

P.S. It would be a big help to me if you told me what you want to know about camp.

Eric in my bunk has translation software on his computer, so from now on I'll be sending my letters in French. Here's the first one:

J'ai un grand temps au camp! Chaque jour nous allons nager. Des week-ends nous prenons de longues hausses dans les bois. Nous n'avons vu aucun ours, mais je pense que nous les avons entendus.

Love,
Neil

One of my favorite games is flashlight tag. The counselors aim flashlights at us and try to tag us with the light. We can only play the game at night. I think the counselors like it so much because all they have to do is wave the flashlights—we do all the running around.

Love,
Nellie

Everything you need to know is on
www.camppinecone.com/eagles/bunka.html

Love,
Dave

P.S. Just in case you can't log on, I'll tell you. We played Bunk B and lost. I scored a run, though!

Lois has an anatummy program with her that has lots of images and video clips. Not everything you told me about making babies is true.

Love,
Rachel

Could you please e-mail me back? I'm having a hard time reading your handwriting, and e-mail would be a lot easier. All the other kids' parents e-mail them.

If you do, I promise to e-mail you pictures of me doing things!

Love,
Gary

P.S. Like swimming, going on hikes and other stuff. We had a hike today to the mountain and I saw a fox.

There's a comic book club in camp. That's good because then I won't want to read any comics when I get back because I will have read them all. Most of them, anyway.

We get to read during rest period and right before sleep. The Spiderman and Superman comics are the most popular.

Love,
Ray

The view from our cabin is great! Thanks for sending me to this camp. I think I would like it even if it wasn't a computer camp. We can see a forest, a mountain and a lake from our bunk.

Love,
Tom

It rained all day and we had bunk rot. Mostly we played cards, but the counselor also made us clean up our bunk in case there was a surprise inspection. They also might inspect our computers for illegal games.

Love,
AnneK35@camporchardhills.org

Very important: I forgot to tell you that I'm in an investment club at school. We each get $10,000 (pretend money, so don't worry) to invest in stocks. I don't have my computer at camp, so could you manage my investments for me? The username is scottg, and the password is moneyman. You may need to read some computer magazines to learn about high-tech investing, but you'll learn a lot from these magazines.

Love,
Scott

I'm learning hula hoop, basketball, and how to swim backstroke. Isn't that exciting!!! I will teach you all those things when I get home, if you want, but I don't think that Aunt Betty will fit into the hula hoop. Maybe there's a hula hoop computer game, though.

Love,
Jeff

Check all my e-mails for my correct digital signature. There's a kid here who's sending fake e-mails.

Love,
Peg

Every other night one of my counselors gets a night off. Last night Mark—he's one of my counselors—came back late and brought a pizza for us. The pizza was cold, but it was real good.

Love,
Kurt

Today was the first day of arts and crafts. I made a pot holder for grandpa, and a mouse pad for grandma.

Love,
Christine

We hiked to the end of the lake yesterday. It took over an hour. The camp bus is much faster, so we hope we get to go on the bus next time.

Love,
Sonny

Here's a list of things I need:

Comics
My Gameboy
My baseball mitt (I've been borrowing Todd's.)
More money for the canteen
A picture of our dog

Thanks!

Love,
Stan

We really creamed the other group in baseball. I hit a home run, and I caught two fly balls. There are some pictures of me on our bunk's website at
www.campbirchbark.com/sunshinegroup.html.

Love,
kid9876

Next week starts Color War. I'm on the green side. Today and tomorrow we're running Color War computer simulations to see who's going to win.

Your daughter,
DiskGirl

As a practical joke some kids raised underwear on top of the flag pole. It was very funny, especially since the underwear was red, white and blue.

Love,
Ian

Remember when you told me about reading comic books under your covers with a flashlight so that the counselors couldn't tell? Could you send me some comic books so I can do that? (You won't get in trouble, I promise!) My laptop screen gives off too much light for me to read without being seen.

Love,
Kenny

You can get the camp yearbook either as a book or on CD. Actually, I want to get it as a book, because my bunkmates can't autograph the CD version.

Love,
Brenda

We canoed across the entire lake this morning. My arms are really tired but I want to do it again. Not this afternoon, though. Maybe tomorrow.

Love,
Lynn

Our bunk got the first place ribbon for cleanest bunk this week. I doubt we'll win again.

Love,
Suzi

There's a boy in our bunk from France. His name is Louis. I'm glad I took French in school, but I still can't understand most of what he says. Maybe you should get your money back for my French class from the school.

Love,
Arnie

I e-mailed you some pictures of me from our camping trip. The trip was great. We hiked up Mt. Jefferson and swam in the beautiful lake on the top of the mountain. And we saw a moose. Do you need any help viewing these pictures? They're really neat! There's a manual for Viewmaster Pro on my bookshelf. It's not a hard program to run. You can also call Mikey who knows how to run the program. I'm the kid in the blue backpack.

Love,
davidm@universe.com

Help! Please send all my computer manuals. Tech support at camp is no better than at home.

Love,
Gabriela

We're getting ready for Color War. I'm so excited. I am going to be on the swim team, the basketball team and the cyber game team. For cyber games we're playing Slime Monster—and I'm already great at this game. You have to keep the slime from taking over the whole town, but it's really hard because the slime monsters can make themselves look just like humans. This week at nature we also learned about the salamanders in the stream.

Your camper,
Beth

Please send candy. I'm not allowed to go to the camp store for the next two weeks. Michael (he's in the next bed) and me reprogrammed the camp computer so that reveille would happen an hour late.

Love,
Andrew

You don't have to send me any articles from the newspaper about stuff going on at home. I can read it all online.
Did you know that the lake is .62 mile wide? And guess what? I swam all the way across.

Your son,
Lyle

P.S. They let us bill our online connect time directly to our home phone number.

I miss you. Would you come and visit me soon? I checked the online airline schedule, and there's a flight up here every Monday and Tuesday at 3 p.m.

I put in a bid for you on Priceline.com. I think you stand a good chance of getting the flight half-price. I'll let you know if you do.

Love,
Hugh

P.S. Bring a few Hardy Boys books. My eBook reader is okay, but sometimes I'm just in the mood to turn real pages.

Did you know that it's really true that peanut butter can get chewing gum out of your hair?

Love,
Jill

We learned a new camp song last night: "Hello Muddah, Hello Faddah." Actually it's an old camp song from the days you were in summer camp. The song's about a kid who really doesn't like camp because there's lots of rain, lots of food poisoning, kids getting lost and other bad stuff. Was summer camp really like that when you were campers?

Love,
Howard

There are three Amys in my bunk. Me, Amy Goldstone, and Amy Wilson. I'm Amy A., and the others are Amy G. and Amy W. It gets confusing when they hand out our mail.

Love,
Your Amy

I need you to send me:

1. Chocolate candy to pay back what I borrowed from Liz in the top bunk
2. My Babysitters Club books to trade with Kim
3. A picture of our cats, Amber and Violet (I miss them so much.)
4. More chocolate, just for me.

Love,
Ellie

We're networking all the campers' computers tomorrow. That means that I can send you e-mails from everyone so that you'll know what all the other campers are up to, too. We mostly went swimming and canoed today.

Love,
Diane

The arts and crafts counselor told us that when she was a camper they used to make ash trays in arts and crafts. I think we're kind of making the same thing, only it's called a coin tray.

Love,
Jay

P.S. I'm not spending all my time in arts and crafts. I'm also doing archery, swimming, canoeing and nature.

There's a telescope at camp. Wow. We saw the Andromeda Galaxy, the crab Nebula, Saturn's rings and four of Jupiter's moons. The views are almost as good as at the Hayden Planetarium.

Love,
Adam

Do you know about bug juice? I know why they call it bug juice! Because the bugs like it so much that they land in the juice to drink! Whoops, if you forget to look in your glass before you start to drink. These are very different bugs than the kind that Daddy yells about on his computer. We don't yell about our bugs, but we try to get them out of our mouths.

Love,
Casey

Don't tell anybody, but Abby has a TV-card in her computer. We get to watch shows! Shh! Don't tell!

Love,
Elizabeth

How's the electricity at home? We get these very mean thunderstorms, and sometimes our computers blank out, which is why I don't write so often sometimes.

Love,
Katherine

When you were at summer camp how many megahertz were the computers?

Love,
Luke

I'm a little homesick. Would you mind digitalizing some pictures of our house and turning them into a screensaver for me? Thanks a lot. I promise to write more if you do.

Love,
Blair

I dove off the high diving board this morning. I was a little scared, but the dive was fun. I didn't bellyflop, which is what I was worried about the most.

Love,
Peter

With all the computers and modem wires in our bunk, it's wires all over the place in our cabin. It looks just like home!

Love,
Alison

I won a blue ribbon at the swim meet against Camp Henderson Lake. Blue is first place! You can be proud of me. Remember last year when I was put in the tadpoles swimming group and I cried? Well, this year I even surprised myself. I want to come back to this camp every year.

Love,
Toni

Don't be mad. I took my laptop on our hiking trip to help keep track of our course, because nobody knows how a compass works and we needed a laptop with a full screen like mine to upload a larger map from the GPS. But the trail was kind of muddy and I slipped with the laptop and it fell into a big puddle. I think it will be okay when it dries out, but I'm not sure. Anyway, it was about to become obsolete, so if I can't get it to work again, can I have a new one?

Love,
Vanessa

About half the kids in my bunk have a cold. It's okay, though, since we're still able to do everything, including swimming. The cold virus doesn't seem as bad as the iloveyou virus that daddy's computer caught last year.

Love,
Crystal

I'm glad that my cuzin Vicky is a counsler here. She's helping to teach me to play socker better, and she reminds me when I don't make my bed before we leave for breakfast. She's grate. She also said she coud help me write my letters home, but I said no thanks. She thinks I need help with speling. I toled her you were used to my speling.

Love,
Rose

There are SPIDERS here. I hate spiders. Can you come here and kill them? My counselor won't.

Love,
Wyatt

Freddy ported AdventQuest to Linux. It's really cool. We don't have a TI here, but it's okay running at 56.6. What's really, really great is that when the server's down, we can run it in protected mode without any graphics problems.

What's new with you?

Your son,
Lance

Tomorrow we go on a hike in the woods. We're going to look at nature, especially little animals, birds and bugs. It should be fun, especially since we're so tired from our Color War games. We're taking along pens and paper to draw pictures of the animals we see, but I told the counselor that it would be much easier if we just downloaded the pictures when we got back.

Yours truly,
Pat

When they say "lights out" they also mean screen savers out, too! It's hard getting used to sleeping without my night light screen saver, but I'm doing okay.

Love,
Leah

I know this is only my second letter home since I've been here, and the session is almost over, but I've been so busy, I keep forgetting to write. I've mostly been doing all those things I wrote about in my first letter, so I could have just copied it and sent it home every day with a new date on it and a note at the bottom saying there's nothing new to add. But I saved you the postage by not doing that.

Love,
Aaron

PS. I still like swimming in the lake the best.

Yvonne loaned me her Backstreet Boys fan magazine. They're cool. Yvonne said you should buy me a Backstreet Boys CD when I get home.

Love,
Dana

P.S. Yvonne is the coolest kid in the bunk.

I like camp more than school. Do you know why? There's no homework. I think there's no homework at camp because there are no moms or dads to check the homework. Everything else is kind of the same, except that we're outdoors a lot more, except when we do computers because the cords don't reach outside.

Love,
Alexis

Not fair! The Blue Team hacked our computer during Color War and downloaded all our team lists and song words. We complained to the head counselor, but he said next time build in better protection. The good news is that we're ahead 55 points and I don't think that they'll be able to catch up even with the stuff from our computer. We're worried about the online game part of Color War, though, because the Blues are cheaters. Keep your fingers crossed for us.

Love,
Dylan, Red Team

Mom and Dad, you'd like this camp. It's just like the olden days when you were young—there's no TV or computers or anything. We even cook things over a fire sometimes.

Love,
Gordon

Here's the order of the groups from youngest to oldest:

Chickadees
Hummingbirds
Wrens
Robins
Hawks
Owls
Counselors in Training

I'm a Hawk. I can't wait to be an Owl, because the Owl bunk has a ceiling fan.

Love,
Tyler

I won my first game of tennis today. The other boy had to quit early because his stomach got sick. But I would have won anyway.

Love,
Eddie

I love baseball, soccer and capture the flag the most. They have computer classes, but I want to spend as much time outdoors as I can because it's so sunny and not too hot. I don't care if I don't see a computer all summer long! What's really neat about playing baseball is that the ball has a little screen that shows you its speed when you throw or hit it.

Your son,
Walter

I need $10. I'm over my canteen account. Could you send me $10? You can subtract it from my allowance when I get home. In other news, they put in a new slide at the lake. It's way cool—all the kids love it. On hot days, it gets hot standing in line, but it's worth it.

Tomorrow we have a big cookout. I can't wait.

Love,
Jonathan

Do you remember how I hate getting up early? Well, I still hate getting up early, so when I'm back home can I sleep late? I've become a very good sleeper. And a very good soccer player, too.

Love,
Carolyn

Today was Capture the Flag Day. This was the most fun day ever. The camp got divided into two groups, the Blue Team and the Red Team. I was on the Red Team. We had to try to capture the Blue Team's flag, which was all the way on the other side of camp. Because the whole camp was part of the game, there was a lot of running and sneaking around. I tried to take the shortcut that goes between the dining room and the bunks, but somebody on the Blue Team captured me. The Red Team won, though, partly because I sacrificed myself by getting captured.

Yours,
Jeb

I have great news. Okay later. Have to go to play baseball now.

Toby

We're not allowed to have unopened candy in our bunk anymore. Elizabeth left a Reese's peanut butter cup opened, and there was a raccoon sitting on her bed and eating it when we got back from archery. Boy, were we surprised! The raccoon kept on eating the candy until the head counselor chased it out with a broom. Our counselor wouldn't go in there, she was so scared. She's from Paris and she said she'd never seen a raccoon in real life before.

Love,
Tina

Jillian in my bunk has a mini-cam attached to her computer, so you can use the computer as a video phone. This means you can see me when you talk to me on the phone, but I'm not sure you want to see me after we've been out on a hike because I'm very messy.

Love,
Amanda

Taps is 6 seconds early. That's not fair, because we shouldn't have lights out until it's really time. I know because I synchronized my computer's clock with an atomic clock. I could really use those extra six seconds to play. Could you e-mail the head counselor and complain? The e-mail address is head@campvermontforgirls.com.

Love,
Jackie

It's really quiet up here. No car horns or anything like that. There's a lot of screaming when one of the kids hits a home run, but otherwise it's nice and quiet. I miss the noise, because it's real.

Love,
Russell

I know we aren't supposed to bring toys to camp, but do computer games count?

Love,
Drew

P.S. This is my third week without any TV and I'm doing fine just like you said.

Camp is exciting. Today we climbed a 5,000 foot mountain with dangerous cliffs. In the afternoon we went white water rafting on "the death river." I think we're going to go hang gliding tomorrow. Maybe not, though, because our counselor said that we have to put our computer games away and actually go outside.

Love,
Emily

It's getting complicated here. Three of my bunkmates have laptops with IR (infrared) ports, so sometimes we make each other's computers do things. It's okay for when we're playing games, but if you ever get an e-mail that says I'm really sick, it may not be from me, so you probably don't have to worry.

Love,
Marco

Remember you told me all about worms and how they can hurt your hard drive? Well, I touched a real worm today for fishing, and I think that I'd rather have the computer worm.

Love,
April

Believe it or not, I'm getting more sleep at camp than at home. They're stricter here about bed time.

Love,
Tracy

I tried tennis here, like you said, and I don't think you need to give me lessons when I get back. It would probably be a waste of money.

Love,
Georgia

Could you ask the camp for its recipe for mashed potatoes? I think you'll really like them, too. What's especially good about them is that you can shape the mashed potatoes into different animals and stuff and the counselors don't care.

Love,
Brady

One of the other kids at camp has the same username as I do, kmmarks. She's kmmarks@interspeedy.net and I'm the other kmmarks. She's Kate and we're best friends now. She likes swimming and the Barbie website just like me.

Love,
Kathleen
kmmarks@technoggen.net

Please don't tell my dentist that I get candy at the canteen every day. I don't think she'd like that. We can keep it a secret, right?

Love,
Jack

P.S. I'm brushing my teeth twice as long, so I won't get any new cavities.

We're supposed to read every night. I think that the main reason for that is so the counselor can sleep.

The funny thing is after playing sports all day long, I'm not so sleepy and neither are my bunkmates.

Love,
Sydney

I know they don't allow any knives at camp, including Swiss army knives, but I've got to have my multi-tool. Some stupid junior camper shoved a 3-in. floppy in my zip drive and I need a special screwdriver to get it out. Can you talk with the head counselor about that?

Thanks so much! When I get back, I promise to help you right away every time when your computer crashes at home. (Except for weekend mornings if I'm still asleep.)

Love,
Mitchell

I'm the ruler of the bunk. Mark was the ruler of the bunk last week, but the other kids elected me. I will be bunk leader for as long as I can keep everyone happy.

Love,
Richard

P.S. Could you send me some candy to give out? That will keep everyone happy.

We had our first camping trip. It was my first camping trip ever. We camped on the field near the dining hall. It was fun, except for the bugs that crawled all over us all night long.

Love,
Stephanie

Josh and I have the top bunks across from each other. We ran a wire between our bunks so we could play Space Raiders against each other, but the counselor made us take the wire down since he kept walking into it in the dark. He's tall!

Love,
Malcolm

P.S. Our counselor is also the camp basketball instructor.

Tomorrow we're going on a 3-day overnight to the Blue Ridge Mountains. Our counselor said that we might see a bear and we probably would see deer, raccoons and eagles. This is going to be the longest I've ever been away from my computer. I know they didn't have computers when you were at camp, but what was the longest you were away from your typewriter?

Love,
Lewis

We're going on a berry hunt. There's a patch of raspberries and we're going to pick them to have for dessert. It will be fun, but I like chocolate more.

Love,
Monica

There was a mosquito in our bunk last night. Nobody could catch it, so we all slept completely under our covers all night long.

Love,
Emma

My sunglasses broke. I didn't need them all last week because it rained all week. But today it's very sunny. Is there any chance you could get me a new pair by tomorrow?

Thank you,
Tiffany

Dear Lucky,

I hope you're having a good summer. You would love camp. There are lots of squirrels to chase, for one thing. For another, there are lots of leftovers and I'm sure that the counselors would let you eat them because you're so cute. Another thing you'd like is the lake—you could do the dog paddle while the kids swam around. I bet the kids would even play frisbee with you in the lake.

I hope that Mom and Dad are walking you every day and playing with you a lot. I'll tell them they should!

Love,
Anna

I've had the chicken pox, right? The reason I ask is that Elizabeth got sent home today because she came to camp with the chicken pox. Just in case, maybe you shouldn't leave for your trip to Europe right yet.

Love,
Colin

I wish the horses were robots. They really stink! I like the horses in my Paint and Play Pony computer program better because they don't attract flies.

Love,
Phoebe

I have the neatest dreams at camp. I dreamed last night that I was floating in the clouds and that I dived from the clouds right into the lake.

Don't worry—I won't try that for real.

Love,
Kathy

Nobody uses an umbrella at camp. It doesn't look cool. So I gave mine away to a girl from the camp across the lake. She said nobody gets teased there for having an umbrella. But you could send me a rain hat. All the guys wear hats when it's raining. Something with a brim that you can snap up when it's not raining. I saw one in that Crocodile Dundee movie. Send it overnight express, if you can, because it's been raining pretty much non-stop since I got here.

Love,
Simon

I buried a comic book on the far side of my cabin in the woods. I want to come back in 10 years and dig it up.

Love,
Ted

P.S. Don't tell anyone on visiting day or they might try to dig it up before then.

At nature class we did an experiment to measure how much it rains here a week. Last week it rained 2 inches. We collected the rain in tubes we made and put inch marks on. How much rain did you get at home?

Love,
Connie

P.S. All our other classes were canceled due to rain. The main field is flooded. But I am learning a lot about meteorology.

Today Nicole got a care package from home with lots of cookies and some candy. The rules are she has to share with everyone but I suspect she's stashed some of it away. If you sent me a care package, I really would share it (though I might keep a little from Nicole, just to get even).

Love,
Brianna

By accident, yesterday I sent you a letter that Peter wrote to his parents. Peter sent my letter by mistake, too. Could you call Peter's parents to switch letters. I think we both wrote mostly the same things, anyway.

Love,
Dixon

We took a bus trip to the lake on the other side of Tumbledown Mountain. From there we hiked to the top of the mountain. We could see all the way to camp from the top. That was the coolest thing I've ever done!

Love,
Ginger

We get to go to the camp store once a week. They've got things like tooth brushes, water bottles, ponchos and candy. But no computer games. That's okay—the money you put in my canteen account wouldn't pay for a single game.

Love,
Doug

There's a rule in camp against magnets. This is a computer camp, so you can guess why.

Love,
Asher

P.S. If you're going on a camping trip you're allowed to take a compass along, even though it's magnetic.

I now like taking showers more than baths. But I still can use my bath toys in the shower, okay?

Love,
Muffy

Would it be okay if we hung the camp flag on our front porch?

Love,
Shannon

P.S. It's a great camp, so you should.

I caught a fish! I did! We let it go in the lake because we were having hamburgers tonight. But it was lots of fun. Mommy wouldn't have liked the worm part. It took about 10 minutes then the fish bit on the worm and hook. Can we go fishing when I get back?

Love,
Jenna

Camp is great! I love sports, especially swimming. The food is yummy, too, especially when they give us extra desserts. But we have to eat quickly to get an extra dessert because there usually are only two extras.

Love,
Bob

There's no fizzy water here. But if you shake your water bottle hard enough, you can turn it into sparkling water. I thought you'd like to know, so you don't have to spend money on Perrier.

Love,
Renee

P.S. It's very hot in the sun and we drink a lot of water!

The baby chicks hatched in the Nature building. They're so cute! We were incubating the eggs for most of the summer and now we have babies.

Somebody said we should keep them hidden from the kitchen staff, so we're not spreading the word around too much, just in case.

Love,
Bridget

Our counselor plays the guitar. She plays folk songs and the Beatles. I really love some of the songs she's taught me. Have you heard of the Beatles?

Love,
Cindy

There's a lot I like about camp, but there's just one thing wrong with it. NO AIR CONDITIONING! It's like the Amazonian jungle in here sometimes. I can't understand why they can't just stick a small window air conditioner in the window. It would really go a long way toward making the camp more comfortable. Do you think you could suggest it to the camp's director? (I'm afraid he wouldn't listen to a suggestion coming from a camper.)

Love,
Jason

We had a dance with Camp Wanakeebana. It was a girls' camp. The boys danced with the girls and the girls danced with the boys. It was kind of nice, but I think I like swimming and hiking more.

Love,
Chuck

Today was Field Day. There was a lot of running around. I'm too tired to write any more letters today, so could you please copy this one four times and mail it to my grandparents, and Aunt Jeanne and Uncle Burt, and my friends Michael and Nate? I'm going to sleep right now.

Love,
Oliver

How's the market? They don't tell us anything about the stock market at camp.

Love,
Harry

P.S. I'm selling all my extra candy for a real profit.

I guess I'm not a vegetarian any more. It's hard to be a vegetarian at camp, especially at the wiener roast.

Love,
Eleanor

I'm glad you packed an extension cord. My bunkbed is the farthest away from the outlet and it's a big help.

Love,
Carter

I'm getting to be a really good horseback rider. I can canter and gallop. I think we should get a horse so that I can practice. We can keep the horse in the garage. And it can eat the grass so Daddy doesn't have to mow the lawn anymore.

Love,
Wendy

I like camp a lot so far. I like my counselor and my classes and my bunkmates. We're doing a lot of fun things, but I'm writing this letter in draft mode in case things change.

Love,
Tim

The grass here is more comfortable than the couch in our family room.

Love,
Becky

The main cabin where we have our meals is painted bright red. Can we paint our house bright red, too?

Love,
Ginny

Last night was movie night. We saw King Kong. It was scary. Some of the kids went into the dining room during the movie. I stayed and watched, but I covered my eyes during parts. Movie night is fun, even when it's a scary movie.

Love,
Cal

Is fishing really a sport like baseball, basketball and soccer? We went fishing, but I didn't do much except sit around on the dock. The rod wasn't that heavy, either. I kind of had the idea when I signed up for it that it was going to be like deep-sea fishing, with a boat, and big swordfish or something. So far all that's happened is some kid caught something that looked like a big goldfish—but he threw it back. I'm going to find out if there's some other type of fishing that's more athletic for me to learn.

Love,
Ernest

A deer ran into the main cabin where we have our meals. I didn't see the deer, but the people who did said that it ran around and knocked over chairs until the deer finally found the door again. Wow. I would love to have seen that, but I guess I'm glad I wasn't in the building at the time.

Love,
Melissa

We're not allowed to have Gameboys at camp. If I told you how, could you download and send me some games for my Palm Pilot (which we're allowed to have)?

Love,
Rod

Can I go to camp instead of school? There's a lot more to do at camp.

Love,
Carol

I told you a computer would be handy! Today we used my computer to map out a rute for our hike on Mt. Plezant. We got the hights, vallies and other feeturs so that we would know where to walk. We also got the wether information, and UV forcast. When we were finished colecting all that information there wasn't any time left to clime the mountain, so we're going to do that tommorrow.

Love,
Nick

P.S. The spellchecker on my program dosen't seem to be working anymore.

The stars at night are much better here at camp than they are at home. I saw the Milky Way and the Andromeda galaxy. How come we don't have stars like that in New York City?

Love,
Isaac

I hit a tennis ball into a hornet's nest by accident. I never knew my counselor could run so fast! It was just like in one of those cartoons, with a whole swarm chasing her down to the lake. Then she jumped in with her clothes on. I wish I had my digital camera, so I could have taken pictures and posted them on our camp website.

Love,
Chloe

Does your office computer let you display hi-rez grafiks? The reason I ask is that I'm doing my art project with fractals on computer, and it would be a big help if I could just send you a disk.

Love,
Claire

P.S. I can make a key chain if you want, instead.

Next summer do I have to go to camp? I can do all the activities from my home computer and you can save all that money.

Your camper,
Jon

Dear Me,

This has to be my last letter home, because today is the last day of camp. By the time it's delivered I will already be home. In fact, I will have opened it and I will be standing by the mailbox reading it. Hello, me! Do you miss camp? Or are you glad to be home? Don't write back, because there will be nobody here to answer you!

Love,
Me

About the Author

Bill Adler, Jr., is the president of Adler & Robin Books, a literary agency and book packaging company. He is the author of numerous books including *365 Things to Do With Your Kids Before They're Too Old to Enjoy Them*, *Outwitting Squirrels*, *Outwitting Deer*, *Outwitting Toddlers*, *Outwitting Critters* (a selection of Literary Guild and Book-of-the-Month Club), and *Baby-English: A Dictionary for Interpreting the Secret Language of Infants*.

Bill was a camper at Camp Wildwood in Bridgton, Maine, in the 1960s. He is also a former camp counselor.

Bill lives in Washington, D.C., with his wife and two daughters, who are carrying on the summer camp tradition by writing wonderful letters from camp. His website is www.adlerbooks.com.